S DOG Says

By John Barker

Illustrations by David Cole Wheeler

PETER PAUPER PRESS, INC.
White Plains, New York

Translated from dog speak by
Jen Gazzo, Barbara Paulding,
and Virginia Reynolds

Designed and Illustrated by
David Cole Wheeler

Copyright © 2011
Peter Pauper Press, Inc.
202 Mamaroneck Avenue
White Plains, NY 10601
ISBN 978-1-4413-0578-7
Printed in China
7 6 5 4 3

Visit us at www.peterpauper.com

On How This Book Came to Be

I'm 30-something, and live with my 75-year-old (in dog years) dog.

He was allergic to my girlfriend, so she moved out. Now it's just the two of us, kibbles, and beer.

He's an awesome dog—kind of like Nietzsche if he'd been furry and prone to sniffing butts. I write down the sh*t he says, and here it is. If you don't think your dog says sh*t, maybe you need to listen a little closer.

—J.B.

You call them
parking meters.
I call them
pay toilets.

You know what "dog"
spells backwards?

That's right!

Now accepting burnt
offerings of bacon.

You see litter box . . .
I see Tootsie Roll buffet.

So when you fake-throw the ball, you think you're pretty smart for fooling a dog?

Do you know why dogs
lick their butts?
Because they can.
NOW who feels superior?

I'm not tripping you.

I'm just bringing you
down to my level.

If you blame the fart on me
one more time I'm going to
hump your leg the next time
you bring home a girl.
No wait . . . I'll hump *her* leg.

Just because I can't
read your stupid clocks
doesn't mean I don't know
what time it is.

Balancing food on my nose = not funny. Thinking you're a dog whisperer = funny!

Don't know why you don't sniff crotches. It'd save a lot of time weeding out bad dates.

Let me explain this to you.
Dogs have fur. We do not
need clothing.

You can thank me for barking so hard that the garbage man doesn't steal even MORE of our stuff. Donations appreciated.

Succumb to the power
of my soft underbelly.

It was your idea
to stand between me
and the hydrant.
Not . . . my . . . fault.

Errors have been made.
Cats will be blamed.

How does it make sense to make your dog, with hearing 10 times more sensitive than yours, wear jingling crap on his collar?

You know why I like to take walks? So I can smell things you never touched.

Throw the ball!
Throw the ball!
Throw the ball!
Throw the ball!
Throw the ball! . . .

Throw the *freakin'* ball!

Can't hear.
Chasing deer.

One dog's poop
is another dog's treat.

Blah blah blah.
Just scratch my ass,
will ya?

I'm not rolling in sh*t;
I'm rubbing off that
stinky shampoo.

Fire hydrant: It's where we get our news.

Not my fault I ate your sock.
On floor, will eat.

If it fits in my mouth,
I'm eating it.

What the HELL is going on
up there on the bed?!

You have two hands.
One for petting, the other
for whatever you're wasting
time with that doesn't
involve me.

Cute beam on stun.
FIRE!

If I didn't "bark my friggin' head off," the UPS man would have KILLED us by now.

Don't be fooled.
The cat IS evil.

My job is to protect.
Your job is to serve.

ME.

Let me out let me out let me out let me out let me out.

Let me in let me in let me in let me in let me in.

I don't care what you feed ME. Whatever YOU'RE having is better.

Oh, like YOU'VE never
drooled, hurled,
or humped?

I'm not drinking from the toilet. YOU'RE using MY water bowl for a crapper.

I dig because I can.

The laser pointer
is not funny.

Nothing beats the
feeling of jowls flapping
in the wind.

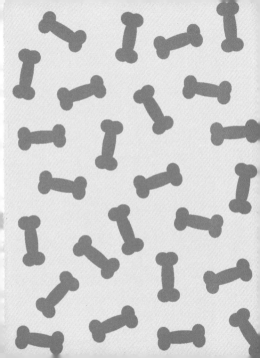

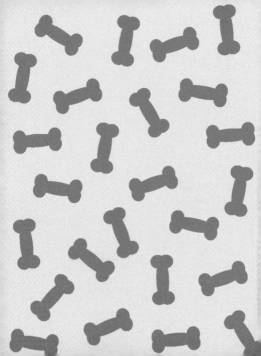